A Tale of Two Squirrels

Written by Kerrie Shanahan

Illustrated by Meredith Thomas

Contents

Cast of characters

Narrator

Squirrel 1 – Sid

Squirrel 2 – Pippa

Acorn woodpecker

Beaver

Pika

Chorus
(all characters together)

Act 1: Summer fun

Narrator: Once there was a squirrel called Sid who lived in a tall tree. In the tree next door lived another squirrel. Her name was Pippa.

Sid: What a beautiful day! I think I'll play all day. Who wants to play with me?

Pippa: I'll play with you. The sun's shining and there's lots of food to eat. Let's play together.

Narrator: Sid and Pippa had other friends who lived nearby.

Pika: I like to play on sunny days. I can roll down the hill through the grass.

Beaver: I like to play in the water on a hot day. Watch me swim to the bottom of the stream.

Acorn woodpecker: I like to fly up in the blue sky. See how fast I can fly to the top of the tree.

Chorus:

In the summer sun they play.
They play all through the long, hot day.
There's food for all in the big, tall trees.
They play and run in the summer breeze.

Act 2: No one to play with

Narrator: One morning when Sid woke up it was sunny but there was a cool breeze.

Sid: What a great day! Let's play, Pippa.

Pippa: I can't. I'm going to get ready for winter today.

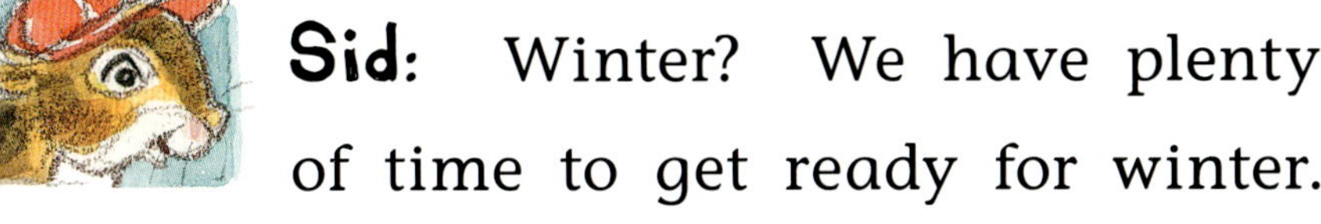

Sid: Winter? We have plenty of time to get ready for winter. It's sunny today. I'm going to play.

Pippa: Well, I'm going to collect some nuts to store for winter. Soon they will be hard to find.

Narrator: While Pippa gathered and stored nuts, Sid went to look for someone else to play with.

Sid: Pika. Pika. It's me, Sid. Can I play with you? It looks like fun playing in that pile of grass.

Pika: I'm not playing, Sid. I'm putting my grass in the sun so that it dries and turns into hay. I will need the hay in winter when there is no grass to eat.

Sid: But that's boring. I would much rather play than work.

Pika: I would rather play too, but I must work or I will have no food to eat in winter.

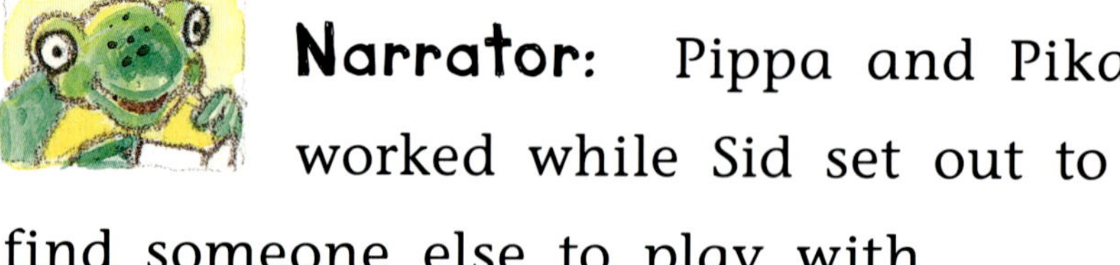

Narrator: Pippa and Pika worked while Sid set out to find someone else to play with.

Sid: Do you want to play with me, Beaver?

Beaver: Sorry. Can't stop. I'm collecting bark and twigs for winter.

Sid: But why?

Beaver: The days are getting colder, the sky is getting darker and the trees are losing their leaves. Now is the time to get ready for winter.

Narrator: The weeks went by. While the other animals worked, Sid played.

Acorn woodpecker:
Peck! Peck! Peck!

Sid:
What are you doing?

Acorn woodpecker:
I'm pecking holes in this tree trunk. I'm going to store acorns in the holes so I have something to eat when there is no fresh food in winter.

Sid: I guess I'll get ready for winter too. I will start tomorrow.

Chorus: They need to work while the weather's fine.
They need to work while the sun still shines.
There's lots of food to find today.
They have to work – no time to play.

Act 3: Winter is here!

Narrator: The next day when Sid woke up it was very, very cold.

Pippa: It looks like winter is here.

Pika: There's a cold wind blowing.

Beaver: Yes, there are storm clouds in the sky.

Acorn woodpecker: And it looks like it's about to snow.

Sid: Well, it's not too cold for me. I'm going to get ready for winter now.

Narrator: Sid spent the whole day looking for nuts. When he returned to his tree he was cold and tired.

Pippa: Oh, my! What happened to you?

Sid: I got caught in a blizzard. And I haven't got any nuts for winter. What will I eat?

Pippa: Don't worry. I will share some of my nuts with you.

Narrator: So all through winter Pippa shared her nuts with Sid.

Chorus: Now winter is here
with cold, dark days.
They stay inside – nobody plays.
Winter is hard but they'll get by.
They all have their winter food supply.

Act 4: A lesson learnt

Narrator: Winter passed, and summer came again.

Sid: Thanks to you, Pippa, I didn't starve last winter. How can I ever repay you?

Pippa: By coming with me and playing with all our friends.

Beaver: Hey, Sid and Pippa. Over here!

Pika: Come and play with us. It's a beautiful sunny day.

Acorn woodpecker: Yes, let's play while the sun is out.

Narrator: Time passed. One morning Sid was sitting in his tree.

Sid: Pippa, I just saw a golden leaf fall off my tree. It's time. I'm going to start getting ready for winter.

Pippa: Good idea. I'll come with you.

Narrator: Soon all the animals were getting ready for winter again.

Sid: Look, Pippa. Look at all the nuts I have collected. And I have saved the biggest and the best nuts for you!

Chorus: They need to work while the weather's fine.
They need to work while the sun still shines.
There's lots of food to find today.
They have to work – no time to play.